ONLINE SUCCESS STRATEGIES

EMMANUEL OKELLO

ISBN 979-888569268-7

Contents

Preface

Today, there are many blogs out there featuring articles and views on as many issues as one can find under the surface of our beloved planet earth. For the purpose of this article however, we are going to concentrate on "how to make money with a blog."

Even though it is true that there are a few people who publish blogs for the fun of dishing out information to the public without looking out for monetary gains, the fact is that most blogs are published for making money one way or the other. For those of us who have been on the internet long enough, this is only a matter of fact.

CHAPTER ONE

A Beginner's Guide To Making Money
Online

Okay, you're reading this because you want to make money online. You are
fairly new to this, so you want some assistance. Well, you're reading the right
article. I will attempt to show you the basics on how to start an online
money-making venture as quickly as possible.

The internet, through its sheer size, can be a bit overwhelming for a
newcomer especially if there are so many different types of lucrative
opportunities out there. Follow these simple steps to get started.

STEP 1: Understand how money is made on the internet

In its simplest form, money can be made on the internet in roughly three ways:

By setting up your own website

A web site can be an ideal way to make money online. However, it should be
pointed out that you have to be prepared to put in a lot of hard work and have
a great deal of patience. Your web site can make money by you offering a
product or service on it or by earning advertising revenue

or both.

You can sell just about anything on a web site but it is recommended that you start with items that are instantly downloadable like software or ebooks. This spares you the agony and extra work of having to specially ship physical items around the world.

You will start by choosing a domain name, registering it and hosting your site.

You need to design a site to suit your needs and what you have to sell. You can use the services of a web designer to do this for you or if you are the creative sort with reasonable computer knowledge and some good common sense, you could do this yourself - it's not that difficult!

You will also need the ability to accept credit card payments from your customers. This has become reasonably easy to do these days by simply making use of a third party processor. Search for these on the search engines.

You then need to market your web site either by way of paid ads or by using good Seo (search engine optimization) techniques to get your site ranked well in the search engines.

An alternate method of making money with a web site is by offering free, useful and quality content that appeals to users. Once you have built up a decent amount of regular visitors, you host Google

AdSense ads. Google will
pay you a commission on all their ads that are clicked on your site. You can
also offer paid advertising to other websites on your own by way of text or
banner ads.

By doing some sort of online work for a company

There are numerous genuine companies out there that offer part time work to
ordinary individuals. You can find research work, taking surveys, data
capturing, typing, etc. You can source these companies by searching for them
on the search engines.

By participating in affiliate programs

Affiliate programs are popular with work-at-homers. An affiliate program is
simply an advertising/marketing program run by a company/website in which
they get members to refer visitors to their site. Members are paid per visitor or
per sign-up or a combination of both.

Most affiliate programs are free to join and the company will provide you with
marketing/advertising aids in the form of text ads, sales copy, banners, etc to
use. It is quite alright for you to participate in more than one affiliate program
at the same time - this greatly increases your chance of success. Incidentally,
affiliate activities create a great deal of internet traffic.

To further increase your chance of success with affiliate programs, only join

established companies that offer well respected and popular products or
services.

STEP 2: Decide what you feel comfortable with

Now that you have a brief idea on the most popular money-making methods,
you need to decide which one appeals to you. Once you have, feel free to do
more research in that area and try to get as much information as possible.

Play around with a few ideas until you are sure what you want to do.

STEP 3: Finding the right opportunity

Once you've decided on what you'd like to do, you now need to find the right
opportunity. If you've decided to start your own website, you need to
determine what it's going to be about. It's best to base it upon something you
have a fair knowledge of or are passionate about.

If you've decided to take the affiliate route or to do online work for a company,
make sure you are dealing with a reputable company that pays promptly. Use
the search engines to find possible companies, then email these companies
with any questions you have. Ask for references (people who are doing work
for this company) and contact these people about their experiences.

Following these simple steps should put you on the right track very quickly. All
the best!

CHAPTER TWO

How To Make Money Online - 5 Things You Should Do

How to make money online for beginners is the one matter that numerous individuals who have a deep background in internet marketing also go back to learn after time. Why is that? Everyone might well expect that those individuals would be well past the beginner's stage but all too frequently that is not so.

Many folks professing to be online business people begin their online ventures in the way they make impulse purchases. They encounter convincing sales hype that suggests they will make a lot of money online without any past experience, training or ability to work hard. Instantly they jump in and then the troubles hit them one after the other.

They have not undertaken the detailed planning to go into any business opportunity. As it is an internet project and because they have heard about so many online achievements it doesn't even cross their minds that they are at the beginning of a very intricate procedure.

Getting online with a family web page in order to stay in contact with friends is

a tremendously different thing to making use of the internet as a marketing

instrument. Marketing, online or offline, is an intricate business tool that uses

the minds of some very creative people.

Does it imply that you ought to give up any notion of becoming an internet

marketer? No; it merely shows the value of proper preparation so let's see

how to make money online for beginners.

Understand how to market online

It appears to be self-evident but a lot of folks don't do it. You absolutely must

educate yourself regarding what internet marketing consists of. Go online and

do some basic research - there's a great deal of good advice about the basic

operations you have to fully appreciate. You could very well start by checking

out Google's webmaster pages which will guide you to other resources.

Decide on your niche

Never attempt to do everything. Constrict your choice of market sector or

niche as that is how to market online and real success will occur faster. As an

example don't try to be a general sports marketer but rather focus on one

particular sport or even some micro niche such as clothing for a particular sport.

Identify your product

Stay away from opting for a product because you just happen to like it. You must do some further research and find out which products are the best sellers. Once again Google makes abundant information and facts available as also do other online sources.

Set up your website

This frightens many beginners but it should not do so in today's world. The processes are far more straightforward than they previously were. Top web hosts and some other sources provide templates that are as easy to use as copy and paste. All you need to do is insert your own product specifics. In fact some of the best web hosts actually explain to you how to market online.

Promote your website

At this point is the place where many folks, beginners plus the more practised, are not able to get it right but there is no real reason why it should be so.

Again it only calls for a comprehension of the multitude of alternatives available to drive traffic to your website.

These include paid advertising and the alternatives which are totally free methods. By that I mean free of financial cost but not of hard work. Lots of prosperous marketers work hard to generate articles for

dissemination online
and use them to bring visitors to their websites.
Volumes of information have been distributed online about how to promote
your web pages. You just have to search for it, study it and put it into practice.
At first it does involve hard work so you must commit time to it. Do not just
jump in without executing the research first. That is the way to failure and
disappointment.
Now then, do you know how to make money online for beginners? You
certainly will when you prepare well.
I have been a marketer for over twenty years and active online since 2002. My
current project is helping people, both new and experienced, to make well
informed choices about making money online.
As an internet marketer you can make money faster. But only when you get it
right. Learn how by getting yourself a copy of ONLINE SUCCESS
STRATEGIES and then you will be on the way to success.

CHAPTER THREE

How to Choose Your Preferred Marketing Method

How do you choose the way you're going to be making money online? This isn't as tough of a question to answer as you might think. There are several different modes of marketing to choose from.

The best part is, you can start with one, and if it doesn't suit your fancy, you can try a different one. You're never locked into anything during internet marketing, so you can keep your options open at all times.

Let's first discuss what methods are available as making money online for beginners options - before we talk about how they're carried out. First, there's the traditional method: Build a website, then drive traffic to it, via either paid search or organic search methods.

Second, there's blogging. Most people already know what blogging is, but all the same it will be defined below so we won't spend too much time on its definition now.

Next, there's affiliate marketing, where you promote an affiliate's product on your own website.

Then there's email marketing, where you use your website simply as a method of collecting email addresses to add to a subscriber list.

Finally, there's third party marketing. Let's see how each of these work.

[1]. Promoting a website: The traditional mode of marketing involves making a website, monetizing it in some way and driving traffic to get visitors. You might promote a product or service on the site, or you just might place ads around your content.

You can monetize traffic with paid search, or you can optimise your articles for search engine friendliness and rely solely on organic search to bring in your visitors.

[2]. Blogging: Blogging is very similar to website promotion, except you're doing it on a blogging platform. This eases a lot of your burden, because you don't have to code anything or build your own website.

You can use a WordPress or Blogger blog, or you can install WordPress on your own website when you try to begin making money online for beginners.

Monetization is about the same as with a regular website, but you might be bound to not advertise in certain ways if you blog right on a blogging platform, due to their terms of service.

[3]. Affiliate marketing: Some new marketers create a very

small website for the purpose of bouncing traffic to an affiliate site. While some search engines frown on this, it is still a viable method of marketing. You should be promoting a decent product, however, or you'll have some very unhappy visitors, and your site will suffer as a result.

[4]. Email marketing: Some marketers develop a small to medium website filled with good advice on a topic of their choice and give away free content in return for collecting email addresses from visitors.

Once you have these email addresses, you can promote paid products to your list and make quite a bit of money on the back end. But this is perhaps a bit advanced if you're learning how to go about making money online for beginners.

[5]. Third party online marketing: If you're really not technically savvy, you can use other platforms, like Squidoo.com, to promote a product. Just don't fill the pages with too many affiliate links, or the site owner might remove your status as an author.

CHAPTER FOUR

How to Select Your Niche

Making money online for beginners is a difficult subject to crack if you're trying to do it all on your own. You likely have no idea where to start. Your mind is boggled with all of the advice you've no doubt read online already.

How in the world do you make sense of it all?

One of the biggest hurdles a beginner has trouble overcoming is the subject of niche selection. This is probably something you've heard of but don't really know much about. I'll explain that here.

Making money online almost always starts with niche selection. A "niche" is a small subset in a category of business interests that you select based on your own personal interests. The reason it's called a niche instead of a category is because it's a very tiny piece of a bigger pie. Let's look at an example.

Let's say you're a big fan of listening to music. In the internet world, you can make money online in that business, unlike the offline world, which is more difficult to break into for that sort of thing.

But you wouldn't want to promote all aspects of the music world on your
website. You should pick just one area of expertise, and focus solely on that
area. You can deviate from it a little bit to include topics that are closely related
if there are only a few products available for promotion.
Using the music theme, you could start your making money online for
beginners' journey by choosing to focus on selling Broadway tickets and
original soundtrack CD's or by targeting a fan base for your favourite band by
selling merchandise and tickets to their shows.
You might even become a dedicated affiliate for a music company and sell lots
of their merchandise on your site. It's up to you; just make sure you don't get
so big that you lose focus.
When you start making money online for beginners, you need to pick a niche
that somewhat interests you personally. True, you can't follow what every guru
says by picking the niche of a product that doesn't sell even if it's a niche you
absolutely want to target.
There's a difference between spending your money and time on something
that will never provide a return on investment and compromising your niche a
little in favour of making it worth your time.
So that being said, when you're selecting a niche, check the affiliate programs

to make sure there are a few that you can use to promote on your website.

Otherwise, you might end up not making any money with your endeavours.

You can even go with an affiliate that is closely related. For example, if you make a website about Tiger Woods, there are obviously no affiliates for him personally. But you can promote golf products or athletic shoes instead, because these are products related to your niche. Visitors will see that they make sense with the theme of your website, and that's the important part.

The 3 Basic Skills You Must Learn

Before You Start

Are you wondering how to make money online for beginners? 95% of people who try to make money online fail to see any significant results because most people don't bother to learn the basic skills that are necessary for success online.

Most people buy into programs that promise to make them a lot of money with no skill required. Needless to say, they wasted both their money and time which they could have used to acquire a new skill.

I used to be like that. It wasn't until I started learning the basic skills that I began to experience some success. Here are the 3 skills you must learn if you want to be successful online.

1) Conducting Market Research
You need to know how to conduct market research. You need to know how to
pick profitable products to promote or develop. In other words, if you want to
promote or create a product, you want to make sure that the product is in
demand. Ultimately, you don't want to sell something that nobody is interested
in buying.
2) Getting Visitors to Your Website
You need to learn how to get tons of visitors to your website. This is just like
any shop in the offline world. If you have a cake shop that sells the best cakes
in the world, you still won't make money if you don't have visitors in your shop.
The online world works on the same principle. You need visitors to go to your
website. As many as possible.
One way to do so is to write articles and submit to article directories like
EzineArticles. You can include a link to your website at the bottom of the
article. Readers who click on the link in the article will end up at your website.
That's how article marketing works.
3) Building a Website
Don't get intimidated about building a website. It is extremely easy when
someone shows you step by step how to do it. You do not need to be a html
expert in order to do so. And you don't even need a lot of

pages to start
making money online. All you need is a simple one page website and you can
start making money online as a beginner.

4 Ideas To Help You Start Making Money Online

Sure there are lots of ways to make money online but you have to choose which strategy suits you best first to ensure that your journey to the top of your chosen niche will be as swift and successful as possible. Here are some of the most popular options to make money online these days to help you get started in no time at all:

Jump on the blogging bandwagon.

Blogging is perhaps the most popular activity in cyberspace in this day and age. Apart from letting you share your passion to other world wide web denizens, it can also be your stepping stone to making money online.

When you generate a lot of your traffic to your blog, it won't be long until companies are going to call dibs on who gets the prime advertising bits.

Whether you're a fan of hot rods or fishing, why not take your passion to a whole new level and set up a blog right away?

Use YouTube to your advantage.

There are already lots of people whose lives were forever changed after becoming YouTube sensations. From teen pop superstar, Justin Bieber, to the entire crew behind the Epic Meal Time cooking show that still gathers more and more fans each day, you might just experience the same success story they went through if you play your cards right. Keep in mind that the more hits your clip receives, the easier it is to convert them into cash.

One man's trash is another man's treasure.

Are you planning to throw away those vintage Deep Purple records you bought in the 70's? Why not put them up for sale on eBay and make money online from home instead?

With millions of users around the world, finding interested buyers for the items you don't necessarily need is as easy as a single click. The possibilities are endless. You may be missing out a lot when you don't set up a seller's profile today.

Promote your business on the web.

Integrating the Internet as a major marketing component for your business is definitely one of the best decisions you'll ever make. Even the biggest companies across the globe are doing it. Why not have the same perks they're enjoying when you get in on the action right now? Next thing you know, you'll be rubbing elbows with the trailblazers of your industry before long.

CHAPTER FIVE

How to Make Money With a Blog

I am sure it would have been a wonderfully welcome experience for many of
us out there to have the opportunity of working from home at our own
convenience, making money and at the same time being able to properly look
after our family members without having to go through the stress of hiring
nannies for whom we cannot really vouch,
Struggling to get out of bed before we actually had the chance to sleep
properly, jumping into the next available train, bus or taxi in order to get to
work in good time so as to avoid the next query from our employer and so on
and so forth.
Unfortunately, not so many of us homo-sapiens have been able to acquire
such a necessary but somehow illusive luxury. So many homes that should
have been happy ones considering the good qualities, Character and nature
of the husband and wife have unnecessarily broken due to the stress of
having to perform their duties properly and earn a good

living at the same time
because of the time factor.
The question that comes to mind here is "how do we then save the situation?"
Or better still, how do we go about working to earn enough money to cater for
our family without having to risk losing the same by being away from them too
long to properly care for them?
This task and how to go about solving such a Herculean challenge is the
purpose of this article. Thanks to the internet, there are now various ways to
face such challenges squarely and one of these is blogging.
Blogging can simply be described as having a one-page site to write about
whatever interests you and your community. This therefore can be done with a
topic in mind as long as it is going to be useful to someone out there.
Today, there are many blogs out there featuring articles and views on as many
issues as one can find under the surface of our beloved planet earth. For the
purpose of this article however, we are going to concentrate on "how to make
money with a blog."
Even though it is true that there are a few people who publish blogs for the fun
of dishing out information to the public without looking out for monetary gains,
the fact is that most blogs are published for making money one way or the

other. For those of us who have been on the internet long enough, this is only
a matter of fact.
Now, having crossed this bridge, the next poser is how does one actually
make money by just publishing a blog? This, I am sure, is the main dish on
our menu today as far as our topic is concerned. I will however crave your
indulgence to allow me the opportunity to put you on hold for a while for two
major reasons:
1. One of my beloved kids is seriously craving my attention to help out with an
urgent school assignment now or never.
2. I also need to give myself some attention since this article is not only getting
too long but at the same time making me thirsty too. A cup of coffee should do
some good as I help my little brat out with his homework.
Isn't home based business such a fun biz?
I however wish to let you know that I am not the type to abandon a ship
midway through a storm. I will be continuing this article sooner than you
expect. Do not blink your eye lids!
I am back. I really appreciate those of you who successfully did as instructed
and did not blink their eye lids although I must say sorry, that you may need to
check with your doctor if everything is okay with your eyes and related
sensory organs. Anyway, that was just a joke. Let's get back

to business

Blogging to wealth is not as easy as a lot of people out there want you to
believe. They are only after your money because they have a product or two
to sell to you. But then on the other hand, it is also not rocket science. It is not
something that you cannot achieve.

The truth is that it needs a bit of dedication and some hard work. If you are
one of those who has been convinced by those dollar hunting marketers that
you can blog your way to wealth without any work, then you are in for a rude
shock. I have been around for a while now, had fallen for such pranks in the
past and know better now and live better now too!

The fact is that just like in the normal job situation, you need to work for your
money. The difference here is that you do not have to break your neck,
inconvenience yourself as much as necessary, and neglect your family in
order to achieve your aim in this particular case.

And so, the next logical question that comes to mind is "how do I achieve all
these things you are talking about?" And here we go!

Please take good note of the following points.

[1]. If and when you decide to blog for the purpose of making money from
home, you need to know that this involves providing useful information and
services to the people who will be visiting your blog. That

also means that your blog needs to be focused on a particular niche for it to succeed. Niches are like special areas of needs.

As you must have noticed by now, this blog is devoted to how to help people make money from home using a blog. This can be described as a niche or special area of concentration. You need to decide on which area you are competent to write on even though you can get articles from some free article sites to populate your blog with. It is always better to concentrate on those areas that naturally appeal to your personality.

[2]. You will need to have some products for sale on your blog. Now, you may start getting scared, right? Well, you do not have to sell your own products!

There are thousands of merchants out there who are looking for people like you to promote their products on your blog and who will pay an agreed amount of money once someone buys their products through a special link that they will provide you with for placement on your blog.

Some merchants stand alone while some are grouped under some affiliate marketing sites like LinkShare, ClickBank, PayDotCom, and so on. All you really need to do is to go to their sites, register with them, select the products you wish to promote (they should be relevant to your blog

topic), get their
affiliate links and place them on your blog.
[3]. The next thing to do is to ensure that people actually get to see the
products that you are advertising on your blog. If nobody is coming to check
on or visit your blog, then no one but only you is aware of its existence. If no
one but only you is aware of the existence of your blog, then no one but you
can buy the products advertised on your blog.
If no one but you is buying the products advertised on your blog, then you
actually may not have realised it, but I make bold to say that you need to take
some advice and go see Doctor Somethin'WrongWith MaBrains while he is
still available and sober enough to attend to you. Anyway, I am sure you got
the gist of the matter there.
[4]. Getting people to visit your blog is also called getting traffic. This can be
done in various ways. You can pay for this by advertising your blog through
PPC (Pay Per Click) and some other forms or you can do so organically. That
is, by spending a bit of your time but not your money.
I am sure a whole lot of us will prefer to spend the time we used to waste on
waking up too early for work, jumping on buses, trams, trains, or taxis when
going to our traditional jobs instead of sitting by the computer to generate

traffic to our blogs.
You can get traffic to your beloved blog to make money by writing quality
articles on related topics (that is what I am presently doing as you can see)
and submitting to highly rated article submission sites like this one you are
visiting now.
You can also do so by creating a list of interested clients though quality
give-aways followed by email capture systems of beneficiaries. You can also
engage in pinging of your blog to the various pinging sites available on the
internet.
[5]. With the above-listed in place, you can then include AdSense links in your
blog so as to ensure that you get some income from AdSense ads when
people click on them within your site.
There are a few more ways to commercialise your blog for money making
ventures but I believe that the above-mentioned ones are some of the most
reliable ones and if you are able work on them, you soon be smiling your way
to the bank without even having to leave your bedroom (or as the case may
be, computer room) to do so.

CHAPTER SIX

How To Make Money With Affiliate Marketing

Learning how to make money at home with affiliate marketing could be one of the best ways to get started earning a little extra cash each month from the comfort of your own home by working on the internet.

This can allow you to continue with your current obligations whether it's your current job, school, taking care of the kids or whatever it may be, while at the same time working on improving your financial situation or even earning enough to replace your current income over time.

It really comes down to understanding how serious you are about learning what you need to learn and doing what you need to do to get really good at it, because unless you get really good at it then you will not make much money (if any) at all.

However when you do eventually start getting really good at it you will see your income surpass your efforts by leaps and bounds. There may even be times when you will wonder where all of this money is

coming from and this is
a good position to be in.
Benefits Of Learning How To Make Money At Home With Affiliate
Marketing

* Less Stress - When you can work from home and set up a good working
environment, it can be much less stressful than a traditional 9 to 5 or office
job. You will not have a boss watching your every move and you will not have
to deal with office politics, unless you choose too.

* Work Flexibility - You will be able to set aside whatever amount of time you
can afford to invest each week for learning and developing your online
marketing business. For most people just by committing a few hours each
week on a consistent basis, they are able to start generating a small income
within their first few months.

* High Earning Potential - Many merchants will pay anywhere from 4%
commissions all the way up to 100% commissions for each sale made. Of
course the higher the price of the product being sold along with a high
commission rate, will yield you the highest profit. However you will always
have the ability to choose which products you wish to promote and select the
best ones for your sales and income goals.

* Passive Income - Once you learn how to set up a

successful and profitable
campaign you can be getting monthly checks on a regular basis as a result of
the work that you did to get your campaign up and running. This will involve
creating or using a good system and may involve building a team or
outsourcing different tasks or projects.
* Unlimited Income Potential - By getting really good at selecting, creating
and running profitable campaigns, you will have the ability to continue creating
more and more campaigns that will allow you to increase your income year
after year.
How To Make Money At Home With Affiliate Marketing
The basic process is simple, you will need to learn about search engine
optimization and also how to do the following 5 basic things:
Step 1. Market Research - This is where you will need to identify a market
area that you will be involved in. For most people it is best to focus on
leveraging what you already know, this could be from your current or previous
profession, training or education or your personal hobby or field of interest. By
starting with something that you already know, you eliminate that learning
curve and move forward faster.
Step 2. Keyword Research - This is where you will learn how to pick the best

keywords for your target audience. Keywords that they are searching for and
interested in getting more information about. By choosing good keywords you
will be able to create good content for both your readers and the search
engines.
Step 3. Content Creation - When you are working in a market that you are
very familiar with it is much easier (and more enjoyable) to create your own
content that will both please your readers and rank well with the search
engines.
Step 4. Website Creation - In most cases even if you have no prior computer
training or expertise this can be done quickly and easily using an automated
website creation process. Using a content management system (cms) like
WordPress is a great option for most users.
Step 5. Marketing and Promoting - When you are just starting out, this is
where you will need to devote most of your efforts, once you get your site up
and running. The more time and effort that you invest in this step, the faster
you are likely to start seeing results.
There you have it, a simple 5 step process for learning how to make money at
home with affiliate marketing.

CHAPTER SEVEN

How to Make Money With Simple Automated Selling Funnels

If you've been researching "make money online" programs, you probably know there are hundreds, if not thousands of programs available. However, there are only a few things that actually work. These things all have automated selling funnels in place.

When you have these online systems in place, things are much easier to manage. In fact, 99% of online business's fail because they don't have marketing systems in place. Let's look at what an effective sales funnel can do for you:

1. They have a high converting capture page. This will allow you to build a mailing list of targeted subscribers that you can offer products and services to.

This gives you the ability to make money whenever you feel like it. See a product that looks like it could really help your subscribers? Make a video review of the product and then send an email to your list inviting them to

purchase through your link.
When you give value before asking for a sale, you can literally print money.
This will only work if you give value first.
2. They have a follow-up email sequence that builds trust with your potential
"buyers." Follow-up emails will show your prospects that you can teach them
something. Make sure to space out your emails.
Schedule your emails to go out every few days. This will increase your
conversions because people need to take time to decide whether or not to
purchase from you.
3. They make it easy to generate leads for your business. Having steady leads
coming into your business gives you the ability to automate your business.
This means you can spend more time creating valuable content to give to your
subscribers.
4. They establish you as an expert in your niche. When you start sending
great content to your list, people will start to see you as an expert. This will
happen over time. However, you can do this quickly if your list is built fast.
Solo advertising will allow you to build your email opt-in list quickly
5. They allow you to live your life and not slave away on the computer. When
you have automated selling systems in place, you have more free time to do

whatever you would like. This is the "internet life-style." When you have all these things in place, you literally have control over the amount of money you can make online. It doesn't take a rocket scientist to succeed online. It takes consistent "daily" action and a desire to succeed.

Focus on the fundamentals and you will see results.

CHAPTER EIGHT

How to Make Money From Home
Writing Articles
Article writers are in high demand as the best way to establish a legitimate
income online. To make money from home writing articles is one of the
simplest ways to create that extra income from the sanctuary of your own
home office The reasons for this are more than one and this article will give
the best of article writing tips for you to get that work at home business going
Video productions are promoted as the best way to get attention on the web.
But guess what -Google can't read videos! This means when Google searches
through its robot system it can only read words and that's why the power of
article writing is still supreme
Content is king is a saying around Internet marketing and the many article
writing services have heavy demand on their work. They know that for every
article that is new and unique the Google machine will be attracted to it like a
magnet. This means that the link on that article will get

good attention and will
be often visited which in turn means sales and referrals.
How do you go about writing a good article with good content? Well the first tip
I would give is don't try to be too original. For unless you are an expert in that
field there is nothing new you can say.
The simplest way is to refer to the many articles already written - gather
several on the same subject and then glean from them the best points to
create your own new unique article.
Of course keywords are so important and my next tip and this is fairly well
known but often ignored is to make sure that your best keywords are not only
in the title but also in the first paragraph and make sure another use of the
same keyword occurs further down in natural way and not forced artificially
which is spamming.
Tips

CHAPTER NINE

Tips On How to Write Articles That Get Read

Article is one of the most recognized traffic driving vehicles to any website.

Beside that, it is one of the most common methods used by webmasters to
get free incoming links to their websites.

This is the "One Stone That Kills Two Birds" method that you can't afford to
miss out on in your marketing plan to drive more targeted traffic to your
websites.

Unfortunately, many webmasters have to drop this useful technique because
they think they can't write, while others may try but fail to generate traffic
because their articles do not get read.

If you are in this situation, you may wonder how to write an article that gets
read by internet readers and drive this traffic to your website by following the
author links of your articles?

The Internet is an information hub where millions of people search for relevant
information. Each keyword search may result in thousands of search results;

the internet surfers won't open each search link to read the content.

They will "feel" which search result contains the information they need and if they are wrong, they will leave the website within seconds.

In order to let the internet surfers "feel" want to click on your article link from the search results, your article must get noticed. Hence, you should have an "eye catching" title and pursuable summary that can draw the attention of your potential readers to read your article for further information. High clickable article titles normally contain keywords such as "Discover", "Secret", "Revealed", "How-to", "tips' & "hints".

When it comes to the body of your article, it should be informative to keep your reader to continue reading and feel like to get further information from you, this will lead them to visit your website.

You may not start your online business in a particular niche because you are expert in the field; instead because the niche is profitable and you want to earn your profits from these niches. When it comes to writing an article about a related niche, you may face problems because you do not know the market well. So, how to write your article?

Well, don't forget that the internet is an information hub; you can find almost any information from the net. In fact, you do not need to be

an expert to write
an article that impresses your readers.
In fact, an article is a collection of useful information and summary of solution
pointers to the problems; you can always find many related articles or
information sites about your niche market. Read their articles & visit their sites
to get useful points for your article, write down about 5 to 10 points that are
related to your article title.
Then, assemble these important points to 400 to 600 words using your own
language and tones; you should have one article ready by then. It's important
to check for spelling errors & correct any grammar mistakes before you
publish your article.
Now, come to the final part: your author link. The fact is people like to get
advice and follow the proposed solution from an expert. So, author bio is the
area where you promote yourself and your business. Let your readers know
who you are and your expertise in your niche market.
Then, tell them what they will get in terms of information or solutions if they
visit your website. Author bio information that has links to free downloadable
informative products such as e-books & guides get a high click through rate
and drive a good massive traffic to the destination website.
So, it's good to give some freebies to your readers in

exchange to encourage
them to visit your website so that you can up-sell them your products or
services.

Summary

Article is an important traffic driving vehicle to your website. And it is the most
effective way to get free incoming links to your website from high PR sites.

Don't ignore this technique just because you think you can write an article.

Article writing is a collection & summary of information searched by internet
surfers and your article will get read if it can provide the requested information
/ solutions searched by these online users.

Nobody is born to be successful as an internet or affiliate marketer, you need
the right tools and useful resources to help you to succeed.

CHAPTER TEN

CHAPTER ELEVEN

How to Improve Your Articles' Ranking

Article marketing is undoubtedly the most trusted internet marketing tool
when it comes to generating traffic and in promoting product awareness.
Writing articles will help you attract online users who are mainly using the
internet for their research.
This will also allow you to show the World Wide Web how much you know
your chosen niche. This can help as people online only buy from retailers
who are knowledgeable or those that are considered authorities in their
chosen field.
The only problem in using article marketing is that due to its popularity and
proven effectiveness, almost all internet marketers are using it. As a result,
more and more articles are competing to get on the first couple of pages of
relevant listings. As you know, your chances of getting your articles opened
and read is very slim if your articles are not published on the top 10 search
page results.

In this page, I wish to share with you some tips on how you can secure better
ranking for your articles to give them that much-needed exposure:
1. Keyword research. First step is to get a list of the most popular search
terms in your chosen niche. Doing this will take just a couple of
seconds. Launch a keyword tracker (use only those reliable keyword
suggestion tools) and choose the keywords that you're going to target.
Ensure that they're closely related to what you sell and that they contain
at least 3 words (long tail keywords are proven to be more profitable).
2. Keyword analysis. If you're not yet considered as an A-list article
marketer, refrain from targeting keywords or keyphrases that are very
competitive.
You don't want to go head-to-head with your successful competitors as
this will surely decrease your chances of getting your articles to appear
on the first page of relevant listings.
Focus your attention on non competitive keywords. Once you're
successful in getting your presence felt, go ahead and target those
competitive ones.
3. Properly optimise your articles. Keep the algorithms of search engines

in mind when writing your articles. Insert keywords on your titles, on
your resource box, on your article summary, and all over your article
body. Then, ensure that you use latent semantic indexing technique
which will surely help the search spiders in quickly analysing the
relevance of the keywords that you're using with your content

.

4. Put together impressive content for your readers. Aside from using
keywords, you can also improve the page ranking of your articles if you
ensure that they're of high quality and very informative. Search engines
are always on the hunt for great articles (they're very rare these days)
that can offer real value to online users.
Also, if your articles are really good and a great source of useful
information, you can expect hundreds of bloggers, ezine publishers, and
webmasters to link to them. As you know, more inbound links will result
in better page ranking.

CHAPTER TWELVE

Tips On How to Multiply Your Web
Traffic

Every internet marketer who's doing article marketing has one common goal;
to increase the amount of traffic that they generate for their website. These
people know that the more people they attract, the bigger their chances of
securing more sales.

Here are very effective tips that to boost the number of your page views:

1. Deliver high quality articles all the time. Online users are sick and tired
of those articles that do not make any sense. So, offer them something
that is worth their while. Ensure that all the articles you publish are of
high quality.

They must not only be informative and well-written, they must also be
content-rich and entertaining to read. These types of articlcs arc the
ones that people would love to recommend to their friends and loved
ones.

2. Write more articles. Strive to produce more articles

compared to your
competitors so you'll get more inbound links and so you'll get more
exposure for your website. I suggest that you make more time and
produce articles that are very short (around 300-500 words).
It will also help if you hone your skills (research, SEO, proofreading,
and writing skills). You'll easily be able to write high quality articles in 15
minutes or less if you're very confident in what you're doing.
3. Share expert information. Be willing to share a slice of your expertise
when writing your articles. Online users simply love reading those
copies that contain information that they would want to know about. I
suggest that you give them useful tips and techniques and help them
solve their pressing issues.
Through this, you'll be able to impress your readers while you establish
your authority in your niche.
4. Use as many article marketing sites as possible. Although it may take a
lot of your time, I suggest that you use as many article directories as
possible when publishing your articles. Prioritise those that have great
page ranking and those that are constantly visited by a lot of online

users on a daily basis.
These include EzineArticles, GoArticles, Buzzle, ArticleAlley, and
ArticleDirectory. Then, submit your articles to relevant blogs and forums
as well. Ensure that all the sites you use will allow you to build inbound
links for your website.
5. Outsource. Writing and distributing a lot of articles to directories and
blogs on a daily basis can be really overwhelming and oftentimes,
mentally and physically exhausting. To ensure that you'll be consistent
in doing the process, I suggest that you hire some people to help you
out.
You can easily find individuals and groups of people who are offering
article marketing services in the online arena. To get great results, sign
up with those who have a proven track record and those who have
in-depth understanding about your chosen niche. Although this would
mean paying them for their services, you can be assured that it's worth
it.

CHAPTER THIRTEEN

Traffic Generation Tips That Work

How Important Is Traffic Generation?

First things first, traffic generation is as important as fuel to your car. Without it
you can't run or function at all. It is the same with traffic generation in your
online activity. Sure, you can pay or put in large amounts of effort for other
things but traffic is key.

Today, you can literally find several places to get traffic from, be it in the form
of search engine optimization (SEO) or just plain leads purchase. Either this or
that there are certainly a myriad of ways to choose from but essentially there
are only a few basic foundational tips to put it to work for you.

Tip 1: Getting Over The Confusion In Generating Traffic Online

Most people actually think it is more technical to generate traffic than anything
else. The opposite is in fact the case, I would say that it is more technical to
set up your website, do any HTML stuff or even graphics or using your digital
tools.

Generating traffic is easy if you know how and it often doesn't have to start
with some fancy software. Sure there are tools out there that will assist you in
your traffic generation activities but you must clear the confusion by investing
in a few good guides on how to generate traffic.
Tip 2: Find Cost Effective Ways To Generate Unique Visitors
Since you're here I might as well tell you upfront that generating traffic does
not have to cost you an arm and a leg too. Oftentimes, it takes only a small
percentage of your time if you do it correctly and consistently.
Now you must understand that just because you know a certain 'killer strategy'
can potentially reap you a great harvest of traffic, that should be your last
resort. You need to first find a method that you can practice without straining
your budget every single month.
Tip 3: How To Get Targeted Traffic Easily
Why do we want to generate targeted traffic? Well for one you don't just want
any old guy to come to your website and then click away. You want that
person to stay, subscribe and maybe buy something from you right?
So, you want to maximise your traffic quality to give you the most benefits with
the same amount of effort, time and money you will be investing to get traffic.

In order to do this you will have to think like a buyer and someone who genuinely has a problem that needs to be solved.

Tip 4: Why Use Article Marketing To Drive Traffic?

First and foremost, article marketing is a very powerful tool to really filter your target market and also to generate massive amounts of traffic. This happens because when someone reads your article that person decides if they like you or not.

If they do, then the next step is to either check out your website or not. What this means is that your article directly separates the wheat from the chaff.

Sorting immediately between the tire kickers and the real deal hungry buyers that have a problem to solve.

Here are More Power Traffic Generation Tips

In this instalment we will go through more details and explanations on some newer more advanced tips to supercharge your traffic strategy. I'll make it as quick as I can hear so if you missed out something please refer to the last page for better introductions.

Tip 5: Spice Up Your Article With Some Keyword Tags

If you are already writing some article or you are just starting then it would be good to take some other things into consideration. When you write articles be sure you spend some time on grammar and punctuations.

In between them, you may want to ensure that your title,

description and even
keyword phrases on your web page are optimised for search engines. Then,
make your articles structured in the same way, just don't 'keyword stuff' your
articles, Google doesn't like that.

Tip 6: Attract More Traffic By Being Yourself

I have always mentioned to my subscribers that if you want to attract people
who like you and that you are comfortable to work with you only need 2 things.

Be a giver and a genuine person.

Create useful content that people can't find online (yes, it is not easy to just do
this but with Google almost anything is possible) or anywhere else. You can
do this by writing your articles from your own ideas or key points. Then, focus
on writing as in your heart you truly want them to succeed or surpass you.

Tip 7: Dominate The Search Engines Effortlessly

Do you know how those top ranking websites stay there even though they
were nobody at one time? Well, let me reveal to you it's because of word of
mouth and a lot of people referenced their site frequently.

Seriously apart from those technical HTML coding and keyword optimization
what you want to do is to be so addictive to others that they want to 'vote' your
site. Get voted often online and you will reach the top sooner or later. It is
better than paying hundreds to maintain your ranking

every month.

About Successful High Traffic Websites

Traffic generation is extremely important for you if you want to truly succeed

online and even though I've said it, it is worth mentioning again. Why?

Because it marks the start of your journey and determines whether you will die

trying or succeed in the very beginning. Without traffic you are doomed to

barrenness.

CHAPTER FOURTEEN

Third Party Marketing - The Secret Tool to Close More Listings and Sales

In commercial real estate you may think that you are the best realtor and salesperson on the planet, but just how will you get that message out? It's called third party marketing; and you should use it to the fullest opportunity as it is very powerful in helping you gain more business.

In simple terms it means that your success with others becomes a story and you use it like this:

1. Get testimonials from happy clients, tenants, investors, businesses.
2. Ask for referral business and follow it through
3. Send emails to your database providing details of successful sales and leasing deals in their area (seek approval from involved parties before you do)
4. Send flyers to letter boxes of successful sales and leasing deals in surrounding streets and businesses (seek approval from involved parties before you do)
5. Place adverts in the newspaper when a noteworthy

property has just
sold

6. Use editorials as a supplement to internet and newspaper marketing
7. Quote clients and testimonials in your proposals and newsletters (get
approval first)
8. Tell stories in your presentations of other clients and prospects that
have been successful in using your services and how things turned out
for them.

This is called third party marketing and it is highly effective in helping you
convert more commercial real estate business and listings. Essentially
everyone likes a story of the experiences and success reached by others in
similar circumstances. It helps your prospect with a level of trust and moves
them towards a decision.

Great salespeople are really just great story tellers, with some knowledge and
experience to help the process. You can use positive and negative stories
depending on the circumstances and property challenge. Third party
marketing is just the use of the experiences of others and feeding that into
your business activities and marketing processes.

It has been shown that third party stories really get the attention of the other
person and they are likely to retain your information better

in the marketplace.
A story forms a picture in the mind of the prospect and lets them know that
they are not the only person with 'property pain' needing help.
Most prospects and suspects remember a relevant story some weeks later; it
makes a better long term impact for you and your commercial property
services.
So what stories can you tell? Try some of these topics to find your marketing
stories:
1. What sales were the most challenging and yet you came through with
success?
2. What leases were the most challenging and yet you found a tenant?
3. What clients had a very unusual problem to fix and through persistence
you solved it?
4. What marketing processes have proven to be the most successful and
why?
5. What other agents or their clients made poor decisions that are worth
repeating to prevent your client from travelling the same path?
This is third party marketing and it is built from the experiences of other
parties. It is no longer you pushing your offering; you have a story to back up
your observations.

CHAPTER FIFTEEN

What Are Third Party Logistics
Providers

Third Party Logistics Providers are firms that ensure customers of outsource by providing services along with their advanced knowledge in logistics and management. Third party logistics providers or firms that deal with logistics and management makes it easy for businesses to focus on their main goals without having to worry about transportation of goods or end line of productivity as well as distribution.

Like said, third party logistics providers will monitor and be in charge of warehouses, transportation of goods, and operation so that businesses won't have to worry about these factors.

These firms would also have to consider market trends to meet customer's demands and needs; it also has to make plans and adaptations for specific businesses in order to strive for profit. Most importantly, these firms have to be closely aware of delivery service requirements for products and services.

Most third party logistics providers add up other services dealing greatly with
productivity, operation, transportation, and other services dealing with
integrating parts of the supply chain which then makes it a lot easier and
effortless for businesses to focus and to leave these factors to these firms that
are advanced and ensured.

Services

As mentioned above, third party logistics providers provide services dealing
with transportation, operation, and mainly anything that involves logistic
management.

Third party logistics providers are well educated and are experienced with
logistic management which ensures customers and businesses their safety
and is something that will minimise stress and will enhance quality in other
areas of business. Other services include:

1. Transportation
2. Warehousing
3. Cross-docking
4. Specific packaging
5. Security system
6. Advices and plans
7. Managerial tips and suggestions

Types of 3PL Providers

There are different categories of 3PL providers which have different jobs and
responsibilities to enhance quality and to monitor as well as

cover all areas of logistics management. There are freight forwarders, courier companies, as well as other companies that offer services dealing with transportation and deliveries. The four main categories and functions of third party logistics providers include:

1. A standard 3PL provider: these providers perform standard and basic tasks such as pick packing, warehousing, and distribution of products.
2. Service developer: these providers will offer customers advanced value-added services such as tracking and tracing, cross-docking, specific packing, and providing a unique security system.
3. The customer adapter: Those providers in this position will have to monitor and take charge of all logistic activities. Most of the time, these people are requested by the customers but they are not included normally in some cases.
4. The customer developer: This position is the highest among other positions with respect to its activities and processes. People in this position will have to emerge themselves and be fully responsible for almost all logistic services of a specific business. Also, they have to look deeply in small details and make sure everything will be done by the time it has to be done.

Non Asset-Based Logistics Providers

Nowadays, technology has now become the number one impact on businesses and the way things are usually done. Logistics management is one of the main areas of business that has been greatly affected by technology and the associated.

Non asset-based logistics providers provide services that still deal with logistics management; however, they do not have to perform on-hands services such as employing trucks, owning physical freights, warehousing, or employing storage trailers.

In short, non asset-based logistics providers provide verbal and visual concepts and services like financial planning, scheduling, transportation fee plan, and other services.

Non asset-based logistics providers are experts that set up teams to cope up with customer needs and wants since they are well-experienced and know technological tools as well as their uses well.

These providers would also learn to negotiate and present publicly to customers their abilities, name types of methods that can be used, and pinpoint benefits the customers would have when using their service.

Though, many 3PL providers today offer transportation services like shipping and flyer service offerings. These transportation services

are called
"On-demand transportation" which has had a great impact on businesses and
has offered numerous solutions to supply chain needs. Modes of
transportation include:

1. FTL, Full Truck Load
2. Hotshot
3. Next Flight Out
4. International Expedited

Possible Reasons of Choosing Third Party Logistic Providers

1. Businesses can focus mainly on other areas of business such as
advertising, productivity, and finance
2. Transportation of goods and its distribution plans are supposed to be elastic
and changeable since it has to adapt to new trend and market changes
therefore, third party logistics providers are needed to confirm decisions on
distribution and to set up plans that businesses might not be able to
3. Third party logistics providers can decrease and minimise the overall
business expenses
4. Business owners and entrepreneurs will not have to waste their time
worrying about distribution, instead, they focus on productivity and product
introduction to the market

Pros and Cons of Third Party Logistics Providers

Pros:

1. 3PLs monitors and provides security for customers and minimise risks that deal with transportation and the distribution processes; some firms monitor places where goods are distributed to make sure all goods are safe and completely distributed with no errors

2. Third party logistics providers care much about their customers and project out their efforts through extra services that can enhance productivity and increase business management quality

3. These firms even monitor routes and ways of transportation as well as use technology to communicate within the system not to waste time and to make transportation faster

Cons:

1. Financial risks and losses- a provider has to learn about a specific business beforehand in order to startup plans

2. Charging minimum prices and costs but add additional fees later- causes customer turnover

3. Some firms may not have insurances for products and transportation systems

Summary

These firms have a wide variety of methods to deal with different customers and businesses which then need time to adapt and to determine as well as pinpoint markets. In summary, the firms provide a safer, faster, and a cheaper way of distribution compared to a business dealing with all areas alone.

People might overlook productivity and logistics management, however, they never knew how important these services and managerial plans are to all types of businesses. Partnerships, corporations, small businesses, and other various kinds would all need a high quality logistics plan in order to meet goals and be successful.

CHAPTER SIXTEEN

12 Step by Step Guide For Your Online
Success-Summarised

Are you looking for the best way to make money online, but feeling
overwhelmed by the amount of information out there? I know exactly what it's
like to be bombarded with emails advertising the latest product and yes, I have
been sucked into buying a few of them.

The secret is to find a simple formula which suits your level of experience and
your pocket.

Here is a basic 12 step process which has been successful for many
marketers.

Step #1 Choose Your Niche

This could be an area you know a lot about or one you are interested in
learning about. There must already be products and services which sell in this
niche and plenty of customers who buy them and are likely to buy similar
products.

Step #2 Choose Your Monetization Model

You need to decide how you are going to make money. There are many ways to do this online and you need to choose one which will work for you.

Examples which are good starting points for beginners are money from
advertising, such as AdSense and income from sales of other people's
products you sell as an affiliate.

Step #3 Build Your Website

You can choose to build a site or blog on a free platform or on your own
domain. It is better to use your own domain as you have more control over
your site. You can choose from a variety of html editors which will help you
build your site without much technical knowledge.

Step #4 Create a Free Gift

To get people to come back to your site and to join your mailing list, you need
to offer something of value for free, such as a report or piece of software
relating to the niche.

Step #5 Get an Auto responder

In order to build your mailing list and send out automatic posts, you need a
good quality auto responder such as Aweber or getresponse.

Step #6 Set Up a Squeeze Page

This is a page which only offers visitors two options - they either sign up for
your free gift or they leave the page. There are no links to anything else.

Step #7 Write Articles

There are many ways to do this and one of the best is article marketing, which involves writing articles providing interesting and useful information on the niche topic and including links to your squeeze page or other pages on your site

Step #8 Write Follow up Emails

You need to build a relationship with the people on your mailing list and you can do this by sending out informative emails which help them answer the questions they have about the niche.

Step #9 Make Videos

Videos are a great way to increase the number of visitors to your site. You can recycle your articles by creating a slideshow presentation and using windows movie maker or a similar programme to create screen shot videos.

Step #10 Create Your Own Products

Once you have learned how to market other people's products, it's time to start creating your own. You can choose to improve on existing products or make products which complement them.

Step#11 Conduct Market Research

You need to know how to conduct market research. You need to know how to pick profitable products to promote or develop. In other words, if you want to promote or create a product, you want to make sure that the product is in demand. Ultimately, you don't want to sell something that

nobody is interested
in buying.
Step#12. Keyword Research - This is where you will learn how to pick the
best keywords for your target audience. Keywords that they are searching for
and interested in getting more information about. By choosing good keywords
you will be able to create good content for both your readers and the search
engines.
The trick is to take it step by step and work on each step until it is completed.
Take it one step at a time, don't allow yourself to become distracted and
focus on these initial steps until you start seeing results. No technical skills?
No problem!
If you have any concerns about what we have discussed in this book or want
to create your own website in no time, and need to find out exactly how to do
it. Email us at emmanuelokello015@gmail.com and we will take you through
the entire process, step by step -

Printed by Libri Plureos GmbH in Hamburg,
Germany

9 798885 692687